W9-BFG-228

ULTIMATE CAR BATTLES

FERRARI vs. LAMBORGHINI

Colin Crum

WINDMILL
BOOKS
New York

Published in 2014 by Windmill Books, An Imprint of Rosen Publishing
29 East 21st Street, New York, NY 10010

First Edition

Produced for Windmill by Cyan Candy, LLC
Designer: Erica Clendening, Cyan Candy
Editor for Windmill: Joshua Shadowens

Photo Credits: Cover (top) by Rudolk Stricker, via Wikimedia Commons; cover (bottom)
DDCoral/Shutterstock.com; p. 4 Alexander Chaikin/Shutterstock.com; p. 5 Massimiliano
Lamagna / Shutterstock.com; p. 6 Robert Gubbins / Shutterstock.com; p. 7 Shamleen /
Shutterstock.com; p. 8 Automobili Lamborghini S.p.A. for Lamborghini, via Wikimedia; pp. 9, 26
KENCKOphotography/Shutterstock.com; p. 10 oksana.perkins / Shutterstock.com; pp. 11, 13
(top and bottom), 14 Wikimedia Commons; p. 12 Shamleen/Shutterstock.com; p. 15 Radoslaw
Lecyk/Shutterstock.com; p. 16 Andrew Bossi, via Wikimedia Commons; p. 17 VT5700, via
Wikimedia Commons; p. 18 Darren Brode/Shutterstock.com; p. 19 esbobeldijk/Shutterstock.
com; p. 20 Fotokon/Shutterstock.com; p. 21 Stuart Elflett/Shutterstock.com; p. 22 Stanislaw
Tokarski/Shutterstock.com; p. 23 CHEN WS/Shutterstock.com; p. 24–25 Kosarev Alexander/
Shutterstock.com; p. 27 Clément Bucco-Lechat, via Wikimedia Commons; p. 30 (top) Naiyyer/
Shutterstock.com; p. 30 (bottom) Stefan Ataman/Shutterstock.com.

Library of Congress Cataloging-in-Publication Data

Crum, Colin.
 Ferrari vs. Lamborghini / by Colin Crum. — First edition.
    pages cm. — (Ultimate car battles)
 Includes index.
 ISBN 978-1-6153-3502-2 (library) — ISBN 978-1-4777-9000-7 (pbk.) —
 ISBN 978-1-4777-9001-4 (6-pack)
 1. Ferrari automobile—Juvenile literature. 2. Lamborghini automobile—Juvenile literature. I.
Title. II. Title: Ferrari versus Lamborghini.
 TL215.F47C78 2014
 629.222'2—dc23
                              2013021162

Manufactured in the United States of America

CPSIA Compliance Information: Batch #BW14WM: For Further Information contact Windmill Books, New York, New York at 1-866-478-0556

TABLE OF CONTENTS

FAST AND FAMOUS

Ferrari and Lamborghini are famous rivals. They are always trying to out-do each other to make the ultimate car! In fact, the companies have been battling for more than 50 years.

Ferrari and Lamborghini have very different styles. Ferrari's road cars are built to be super fast and sleek, like racecars. This is because a racecar driver started Ferrari! Lamborghinis are known for being comfortable, fast, and

Ferrari 458 Spider

Lamborghini
Murciélago

bold-looking. One famous Lamborghini **feature** is the scissor door. Both Ferrari and Lamborghini are known for using powerful V12 engines in many models. They are also famous for their limited edition cars, such as the 1957 Ferrari Testa Rossa and the 2007 Lamborghini Reventon.

Both Ferrari and Lamborghini were started in Italy. The Ferrari logo is a black prancing horse. The Lamborghini logo is a gold raging bull.

ALL ABOUT FERRARIS

Not every car company was started by a racecar driver, but Ferrari was! Their racing history is one of the things that makes Ferrari special. Before Ferrari made road cars, they made only racecars. Since 1947, they have made both.

Ferrari fans like the racing feel of Ferrari road cars. They are built to be light, fast, and loud.

Ferraris are also very expensive. Many models have a base price of at least $200,000. This makes Ferraris **exclusive**, because

2013 Ferrari F12berlinetta

The Ferrari California is one of the most **aerodynamic** models the company makes. The shape of this hard top convertible is **designed** to reduce **drag**.

Record Breaking Prices!

Ferrari has also set many records for the most expensive cars sold. In 2011, a 250 Testa Rossa **prototype** broke records by selling for more than $16 million at **auction**! Then, in 2012, a 1962 Ferrari 250 GTO set a new record when it sold to a private collector for $35 million!

not everyone can afford one. Ferraris are expensive because of their racing design and handmade or high-tech parts. All of these things make Ferraris high-performance cars that people love to drive!

ALL ABOUT LAMBORGHINIS

Unlike Ferrari, Lamborghini does not have a long racing history. Instead, Lamborghini focuses on making high-performance cars for the road. Lamborghinis are designed to be exciting to look at and to drive! While Ferraris generally have rounder designs, Lamborghinis are known for their sharp angles and hard edges. They are also known for their loud, high-horsepower engines.

Like Ferraris, Lamborghinis can be very expensive to buy.

Lamborghini "Charging Bull" Logo

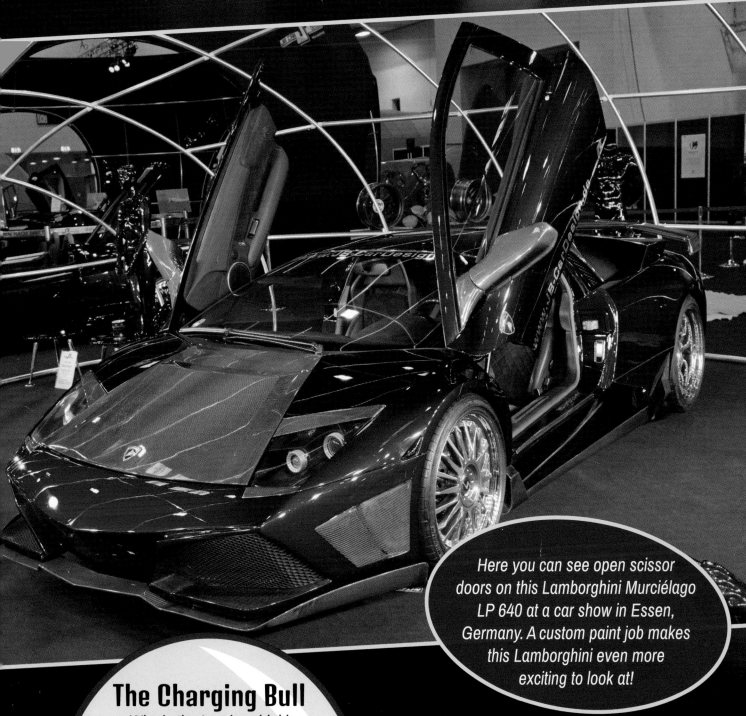

Here you can see open scissor doors on this Lamborghini Murciélago LP 640 at a car show in Essen, Germany. A custom paint job makes this Lamborghini even more exciting to look at!

The Charging Bull

Why is the Lamborghini logo a charging bull? It is because the founder of Lamborghini was a big fan of Spanish bullfighting! The names of many Lamborghini models have to do with bullfighting, such as the Islero, the Murciélago, and the Reventon. All of these models are named after famous bulls.

They are also expensive to build! This means that only small numbers of these super cars are made. Some models even have waiting lists! Both **vintage** and current Lamborghini models can be considered collector's items.

9

FROM RACING TO THE ROAD

Ferrari was founded by Enzo Ferrari, an Italian racecar driver. Enzo went to his first car race when he was just 10 years old! In 1924, he won his first race for the Alfa Romeo team.

Enzo started his own racing team, Scuderia Ferrari, in 1929. Ferrari's first headquarters was in Modena, Italy.

At first, Enzo was focused on making racecars. However, he decided that selling sports cars

Ferrari Enzo

This is a replica, or exact copy, of a Ferrari 125 S built using the original plans for the model. You can see this replica at the Museo Ferrari in Maranello, Italy.

would make money for his racing team. In 1947, Ferrari built its first sports car, the 125 S. This sports car had a 1.5 liter V12 engine. Only three were made!

In 1949, Ferrari introduced its first grand tourer, or GT, model. The 166 Inter was a two-seater with a V12 engine. This popular car was the first of many GTs for Ferrari!

LAMBORGHINI'S BEGINNINGS

Lamborghini was started by an Italian named Ferruccio Lamborghini. He owned a successful company that made tractors. This made him very rich. Ferruccio liked to spend his money on expensive cars. He owned cars from makers such as Alfa Romeo, Maserati, and Ferrari.

At this time, many people thought Ferrari made the best cars. However, Ferruccio did not like driving his Ferrari. He thought he could make a better sports car than Ferrari

Lamborghini Countach 5000

could. He decided to start his own company in Sant'Agata Bolognese, Italy.

In 1963, Lamborghini introduced its first prototype at the Turin Motor Show. This was a coupe called the 350 GTV. The first model for sale from Lamborghini was the 280-horsepower 1964 350 GT. In 1966, Lamborghini introduced the 1966 400 GT. The GT had a 320-horsepower V12 engine.

FERRARI OVER TIME

Over the years, Ferrari has used many different designs. However, all Ferraris are built to be fast and beautiful!

Ferrari's 250 series was known for its clean, rounded lines. Ferrari's first popular 2+2 model was the 250 GTE. It had two seats in the front and two in the back. The 250 Testa Rossa and 250 GTO are some of the most famous racing cars of all time!

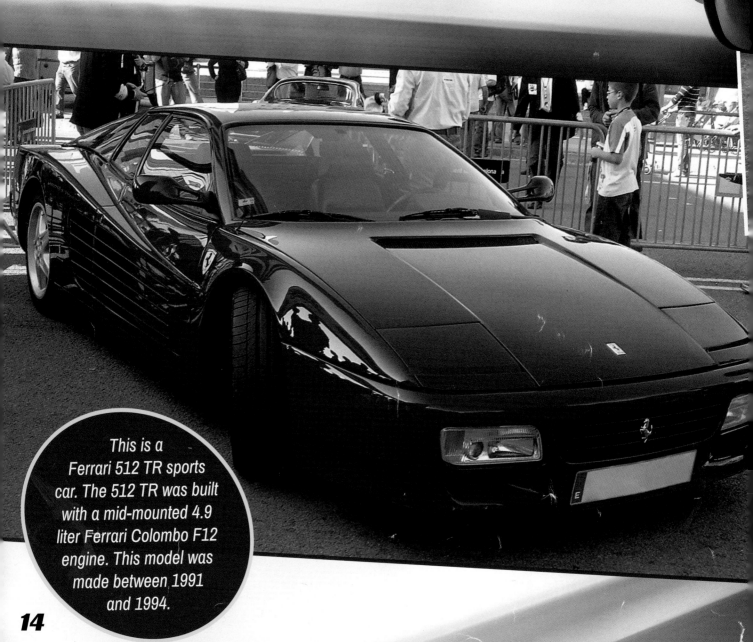

This is a Ferrari 512 TR sports car. The 512 TR was built with a mid-mounted 4.9 liter Ferrari Colombo F12 engine. This model was made between 1991 and 1994.

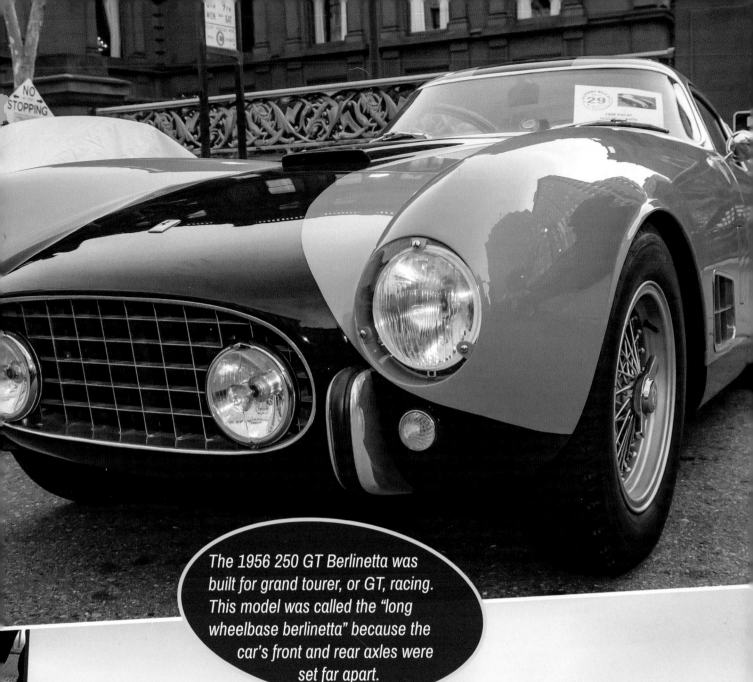

The 1956 250 GT Berlinetta was built for grand tourer, or GT, racing. This model was called the "long wheelbase berlinetta" because the car's front and rear axles were set far apart.

The 1973 Berlinetta Boxer was a change for Ferrari. It had Ferrari's first mid-engine V12 design. The 1984 Testarossa was known for its large side intakes. The Testarossa appeared in many video games during the 1980s and 1990s!

The Ferrari F40

*In 1987, the Ferrari F40 was built for Ferrari's 40th **anniversary**. It was the last Ferrari designed while Enzo Ferrari was alive. At the time, it was Ferrari's fastest car. It was also the most expensive. The F40 had a price of $400,000 in 1987. Today, that is more than $800,000!*

50 YEARS OF LAMBORGHINI

Lamborghini celebrated its 50th anniversary in 2013! Since 1963, the design and **engineering** of Lamborghini's cars has only gotten better.

In 1966, Lamborghini introduced its Miura line of cars. These high-performance 2-door coupes became famous for their mid-engine design. When it went on sale in 1966, the Miura P400 was the fastest road car on the market.

Another famous early Lamborghini was the 1974

Lamborghini Miura P400

This Diablo VT Roadster was introduced in 1995. This model was known for its removable carbon-fiber roof, called a targa top. Targa means "plate" in Italian.

Countach. People were impressed by its V12 engine, scissor doors, and angular shape. In 1990, the Diablo became the first Lamborghini to break 200 miles per hour (321 km/h). The lighter Diablo SE30 was built to be a street-racing car.

Low-Down Lamborghini

The Murciélago was one of Lamborghini's most famous designs. The body was built to be very low to the ground. In fact, the tallest point on the roof is only 4 feet (1.2 m) high! Both 2-door coupe and roadster models were made with V12 engines and all-wheel drive. This line was sold between 2004 and 2010.

A RACING LEGEND

Ferrari is one of the most famous names in racing. They are also one of the oldest. Ferrari has built racecars for both sports car racing and Formula One racing. However, Ferrari is best known for its Formula One team.

Ferrari's Formula One team is called Scuderia Ferrari. They are the only team to have raced in the World Championship every year since 1950! Ferrari's

Ferrari Formula One racecars such as this one look very different than Ferrari sports cars! This Ferrari F1 car was shown at the 2013 North American *International* Auto Show.

Here, a Ferrari F458 Italia GT2 is being driven in the 2012 6 Hours of Spa-Francorchamps race. Teams driving this model have won many races, including the 2011 Le Mans Series.

drivers and cars have won many F1 championships over the years. These include 15 World Driver's Championships and 16 World Constructor's Championships.

Scuderia Ferrari also took part in sports car racing until 1973. They won many titles in the 24 Hours of Le Mans and World Sportscar Championships. Since 1973, Ferrari has built racing sports cars for other teams. Ferrari F430s raced by other teams have also won many championships!

LAMBORGHINI IN RACING

Lamborghini's racing history is not as long as Ferrari's. In fact, Ferruccio Lamborghini did not want to take part in car racing at all. Lamborghini's cars are for fans of street driving.

Lamborghini does not have its own Formula One race team. However, it has made engines for some F1 racecars between 1989 and 1993. These include cars raced by Larrousse, Lotus, Minardi, and Ligier. For example, the

The Lotus 102 F1 racecar, built with a Lamborghini V12 engine, is shown here. The Lotus team drove this car in 37 races between 1990 and 1992.

Here, Paul Stokell drives his Lamborghini Diablo GTR in the 2004 Australian Nations Cup in Adelaide, Australia. Stokell won this race with his Diablo GTR in both 2003 and 2004.

Lotus 102 was built with a Lamborghini V12 engine. This car raced for the Lotus F1 team in 1990.

Lamborghini has also made cars for GT racing. Lamborghini built racing versions of their Diablo model.

These were called the Diablo SVR and Diablo 6.0 GTR. A Lamborghini Murcielago R-GT won the 2007 FIA GT Zhuhai 2 Hours in Zhuhai, China. This was the first ever win for a Lamborghini in an international race!

WHO WINS AT RACING?

Ferrari and Lamborghini both build racing cars. However, Ferrari is the clear winner in racing if you **compare** them. Lamborghini makes very fast cars, but Ferrari's racing history puts them on top. Ferrari cars have won many more Formula One races and GT races than Lamborghini.

You might see a race between a Ferrari and a Lamborghini in Las Vegas,

A Ferrari 430 Scuderia is shown here at the 2010 Verva Street Race in Warsaw, Poland. For this race, Warsaw's streets are turned into a racing circuit once a year!

This is a Lamborghini Gallardo racing down the track in the 2011 GT Asia Series. This race took place at the Sepang International Circuit in Sepang, Malaysia.

Nevada. At the Las Vegas Motor Speedway, visitors can pay to race an **exotic** street car around a track. These cars include the Lamborghini Gallardo Superleggera, Ferrari 458 Italia, or Ferrari 599 GTB Fiorano. Visitors can also drive a F430 GT racing Ferrari!

The Gallardo Superleggera is a super light Lamborghini with a V10 engine. It can go from 0 to 60 miles per hour (0–97 km/h) in just 3.8 seconds. The Ferrari 485 Italia is Ferrari's first mid-engine road car with direct fuel injection. It can go from 0 to 60 miles per hour (0–97 km/h) in under 3.4 seconds! A race between these two cars would be very exciting.

FERRARI TODAY AND TOMORROW

Ferrari's current road models are fast and exciting! The Ferrari California is a 2+2 hard-top convertible with a V8 engine. The F12berlinetta is a super car with a mid-engine design and rear-wheel drive. The Ferrari FF is a four-seater with four-wheel drive. It has a top speed of 208 miles per hour (335 km/h)!

What's next for Ferrari? At the 2013 Geneva Auto Show, Ferrari introduced the LaFerrari. The LaFerrari is a limited-edition **hybrid** sports car. Only 499 will be built. The LaFerrari is said to have a top-speed of 220 miles per hour (354 km/h). That is super fast!

Here, many different red Ferrari racing and sports car models are shown at the Museo Ferrari in Maranello, Italy. Red is the national racing color of Italy.

The 512 S Modulo

The Ferrari 512 S Modulo is one of Ferrari's weirdest concept cars. A concept car shows a new style or technology but may not be for sale. Ferrari introduced the Modulo at the 1970 Geneva Motor Show. Its body was wide, flat, and very low to the ground. The Modulo was most famous for its canopy roof.

2002 - Ferrari 360 GT - V8 90° - 3586 cc

1954 - Ferrari 375 Plus - V12 60° 4954 cc

LAMBORGHINI'S FUTURE

Lamborghini keeps making bold cars for driving fans. The Aventador is a two-seat sports car with a V12 engine. It has a top speed of 217 miles per hour (349 km/h)! The Sesto Elemento is a two-door coupe with a V10 engine. Much of its body is made of carbon fiber.

Lamborghini introduced the Veneno at the 2013 Geneva Auto Show. The Veneno is a super limited-edition sports car. Only three were made. Each Veneno costs almost $4 million! Lamborghini also

This is the 2012 Lamborghini Aventador LP 700-4. This model was built with Lamborghini's all-new 6.5 liter V12 engine and Independent Shifting Rod gear box designs.

This Lamborghini Veneno was shown at the 2013 Geneva Motor Show. It is called Car Zero, because it is not one of the three Venenos made for sale. It is being saved for a museum!

The Estoque

Lamborghini has never made cars with four doors for sale. However, Lamborghini has made a four-door concept car. Lamborghini showed off the Estoque concept car at the 2008 Paris Motor Show. The Estoque has a four-door sedan design unlike Lamborghini's two-seat sports cars. However, Lamborghini has decided to stick with its two-door designs!

showed the bright yellow Aventador LP720-4 50° Anniversario at the 2013 Shanghai Auto Show. Just 100 of these cars were made to celebrate Lamborghini's 50th anniversary.

27

COMPARING SUPERCARS

Some people are big fans of Ferrari. Others like Lamborghini better. Some people like both! Many car fans like to argue about

FERRARIS

Date Founded	1947
First Model	125S
Current Owner	Fiat
Current Models in 2013–2014	458 Italia 458 Spider California F12berlinetta FF LaFerrari
Best 0–60 mph (0–97 km/h)	2.8 seconds 2012 Aventador LP700-4
Top Speed	220 miles per hour (354 km/h) 2013 LaFerrari
Most Expensive Sales Price	$1.3 million 2013 LaFerrari
Best-Selling Model	360 Over 17,000 sold
Cars Sold in 2012	7,318 cars sold

whether Ferrari or Lamborghini makes better cars. This can be difficult because they have different styles. You can look at **statistics** to help you compare Ferrari and Lamborghini!

LAMBORGHINIS

Date Founded	1963
First Model	350 GTV
Current Owner	Volkswagen
Current Models in 2013–2014	Aventador LP 700-4 Aventador LP 700-4 Roadster Gallardo LP 560-4 Gallardo LP 560-4 Spyder Sesto Elemento Veneno
Best 0–60 mph (0–97 km/h)	2.8 seconds 2005 FXX Enzo
Top Speed	220 miles per hour (354 km/h) 2013 Veneno
Most Expensive Sales Price	$4.9 million 2013 Veneno
Best-Selling Model	Gallardo Over 10,000 sold
Cars Sold in 2012	2,083 cars sold

YOU DECIDE!

Ferrari and Lamborghini both have many fans. These rivals are two of the best supercar makers in the world! Ferraris and Lamborghinis are famous for being fast and expensive. Which do you like better?

Do you like sleek and beautiful cars built like race cars? If so, Ferrari may be for you! Do you like fast, bold-looking cars built for comfort? If so, you might be a fan of Lamborghini! Only you can decide who makes the best supercar.

Ferrari Enzo

Lamborghini Superleggera

GLOSSARY

aerodynamic (er-oh-dy-NA-mik) Made to move through the air easily.

anniversary (a-nuh-VERS-ree) The date on which an event occurred in the past or its special observance.

auction (OK-shun) A sale at which goods are sold to whoever pays the most.

compare (kum-PER) To see how two or more things are alike or unlike.

designed (dih-ZYND) Conceived or formed the plan for something.

drag (DRAG) A force that goes against the motion of an object as the object tries to move through a gas or a liquid.

engineering (en-juh-NIR-ing) The work that uses scientific knowledge for practical things, such as designing machines.

exclusive (ek-SKLOO-siv) Limited to a single individual or group.

exotic (ig-ZAH-tik) Strange or unusual.

feature (FEE-chur) The special look or form of people or objects.

hybrid (HY-brud) Cars that have an engine that runs on gasoline and a motor that runs on electricity.

international (in-tur-NA-shuh-nul) Having to do with more than one country.

prototype (PROH-tuh-typ) The first model on which later models are based.

statistics (stuh-TIS-tiks) Facts in the form of numbers.

vintage (VIN-tij) Dating from long ago.

FURTHER READING

Martin, Michael J. *The World's Fastest Cars*. The World's Top Tens. Mankato, MN: Capstone Press, 2006.

Power, Bob. *Ferraris*. Wild Wheels. New York: Gareth Stevens Learning Library, 2011.

Quinlan, Julia J. *Lamborghini*. Speed Machines. New York: PowerKids Press, 2012.

INDEX

WEBSITES

For web resources related to the subject of this book, go to:
www.windmillbooks.com/weblinks
and select this book's title.